30 Amazing Facts About Zebras

Sarah Hawkins

Copyright © 2017 Sarah Hawkins

All rights reserved.

ISBN:
ISBN- 9781521704943

DEDICATION

This book is dedicated to my two Sons who love facts and animals.

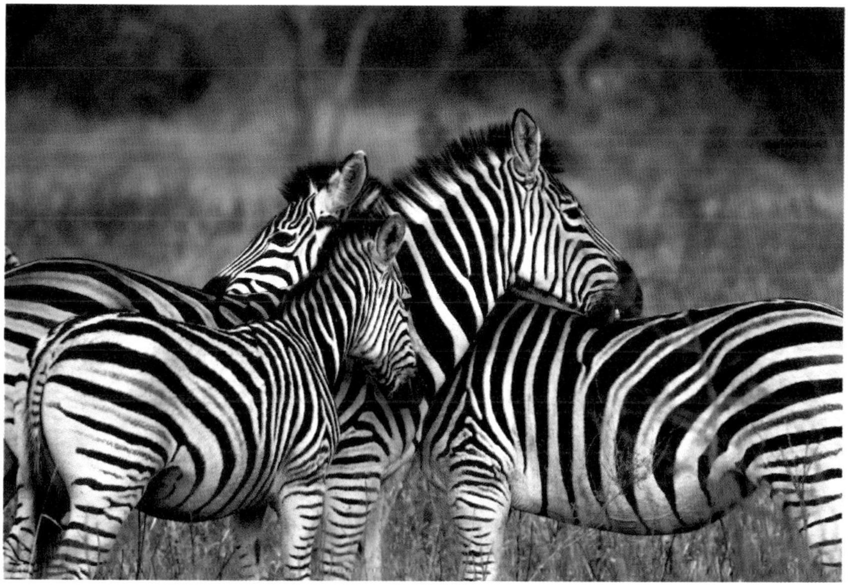

There's no limit to how much you'll know, depending how far beyond zebra you go.

Dr. Seuss

Did you know that there are three species of Zebras?

The three species of Zebra are called the 'Plains Zebra', the 'Grevy's Zebra' and the 'Mountain Zebra'.

They all live in different areas of Africa.

PLAINS ZEBRAS

1) A Plains Zebra is sometimes called a common zebra, painted zebra or a Burchell's.

2) The scientific name for a Plains Zebra is Equus quagga.

3) A Plains Zebra weighs between 175 to 385 kilograms.

4) Plains Zebras live in East and South Africa in areas of woodland and in open grasslands where there are no trees.

Sarah Hawkins

A PLAINS ZEBRA

GREVVY'S ZEBRA

5) A Grevy's Zebra lives in Ethiopia and Northern Kenya.

6) A Grevy's Zebra is sometimes called an Imperial Zebra.

7) Its scientific name is Equus grevyi.

8) Grevy's Zebras are an endangered species due to being hunted for their skin. Habitat loss which has been caused due to overgrazing has caused a threat to the survival of these Zebras

9) There are approximately only 2000 Grevy's Zebras left on the planet.

10) A Grevy Zebra can live without water for up to 5 days.

11) A Grevy Zebra can live without water for up to 5 days.

12) A Grevy Zebra is pregnant for 13 months.

ALL SPECIES OF ZEBRA FACTS

13) Zebras all have different patterns of stripes.

14) A male Zebra is a Stallion.

15) A female Zebra is a Mare.

16)A Zebra can run up to 40mph.

17)A Zebra usually sleeps standing up.

18)When a Zebra is being chased by a predator they run in a zig zag pattern to make it difficult for the predator to catch them.

19)Zebra's predators are Lions, Cheetahs, Hyenas, Leopards and Humans.

20)Zebras are more active in the daylight. They spend half of this time feeding.

21)Zebras are herbivores and eat grass, shrubs, leaves, twigs and sometimes bark from trees.

22)Under the Zebras black and white stripes its skin is black.

23)Zeal is the name for a group of Zebras.

24)When a Zebra a foal is born, the mother keeps the foal away from the other Zebras so it can learn its mothers voice, smell and appearance.

25)When a Zebra is born, it has brown and white stripes. The brown stripes will turn back when the foal is between 9 to 18 months old.

26)Every year Zebras trek over 1,800 miles during the Great Migration.

MOUNTAIN ZEBRAS

27)A Mountain Zebra lives in Namibia, Angola and South Africa.

28)Mountain Zebras are excellent climbers and live in hilly and mountainous areas.

29)Mountain Zebras don't live in a large herd like Plain Zebras. They live in a herd of up to 6.

30)A Mountain Zebras ears are very pointy and can grow up to 8 inches. Their tail is an average length of 20 inches.

WHAT DID YOU LEARN ABOUT ZEBRA'S?

Questions

A) What is a female Zebra called?

B) What is a male Zebra called?

C) Where do Plains Zebras live?

D) What is a group of Zebras called?

E) How many miles does a Zebra trek every year during the Great Migration?

F) What colour is a Zebra's skin?

G) Do Zebras all have the same stripes?

H) What time of the day are Zebras the most active?

I) What do Zebras eat?

J) How does a Zebra sleep?

K) How long can a Grevy's Zebra go without drinking any water?

L) How fast can a Zebra run?

ANSWERS

A) Mare

B) Stallion

C) Plains Zebras live in East and South Africa in areas of woodland and in open grasslands where there are no trees.

D) Zeal

E) 1800 Miles

F) Black

G) No, every Zebra has a unique pattern of stripes.

H) Daytime

I) Zebras are herbivores and eat grass, shrubs, leaves, twigs and sometimes bark from trees.

J) Standing up.

K) 5 days.

L) Up tom 40mph.

ABOUT THE AUTHOR

Sarah Hawkins is a Mother of two boys. She is a freelance writer and photographer based in Derbyshire. Sarah loves travelling, writing and learning new things.

Sarah Hawkins

30 Amazing Facts About Zebras

Sarah Hawkins

30 Amazing Facts About Zebras

Sarah Hawkins

30 Amazing Facts About Zebras

Printed in Great Britain
by Amazon